Summer Flowers
Coloring Book
By
Harlo Books

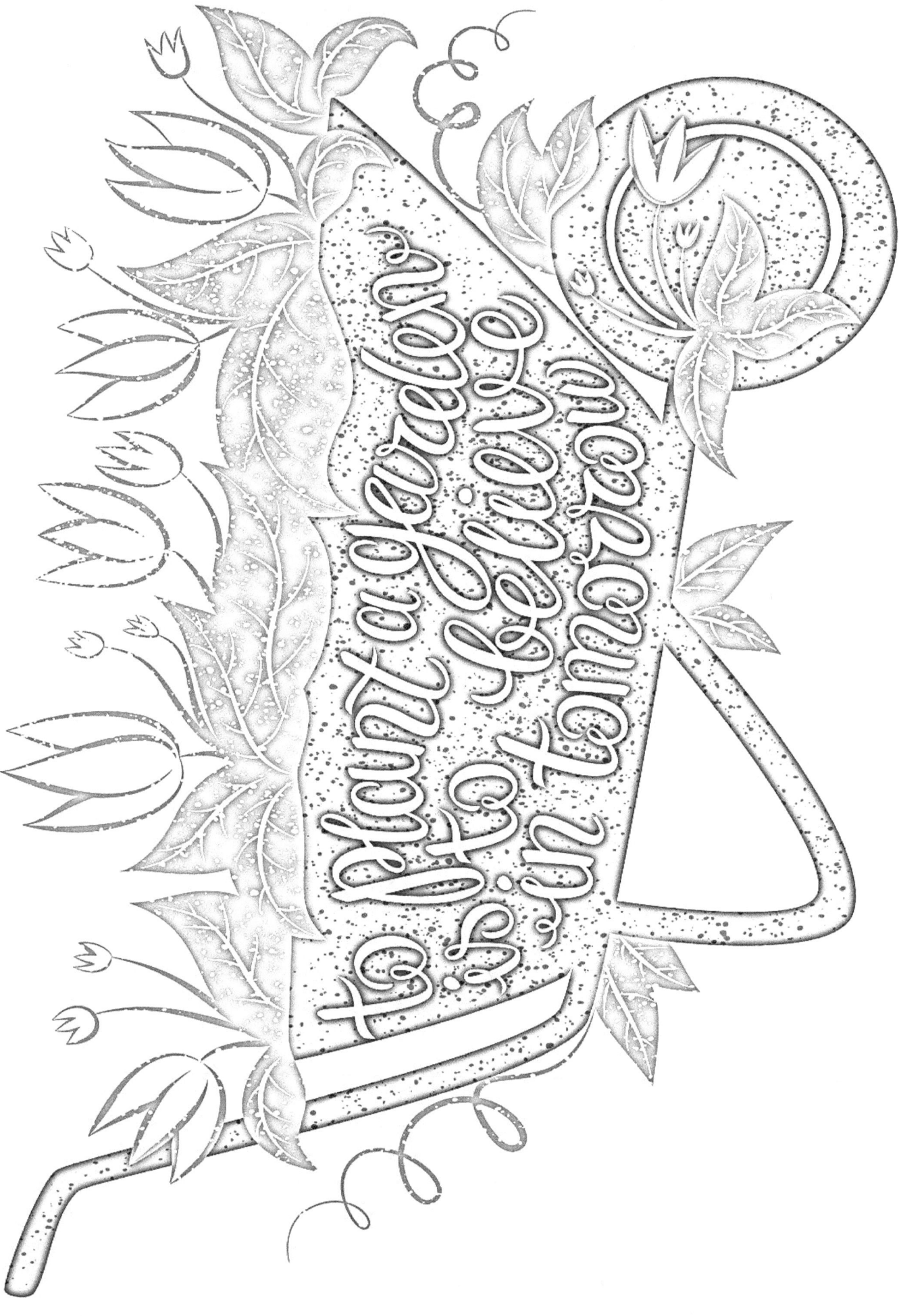

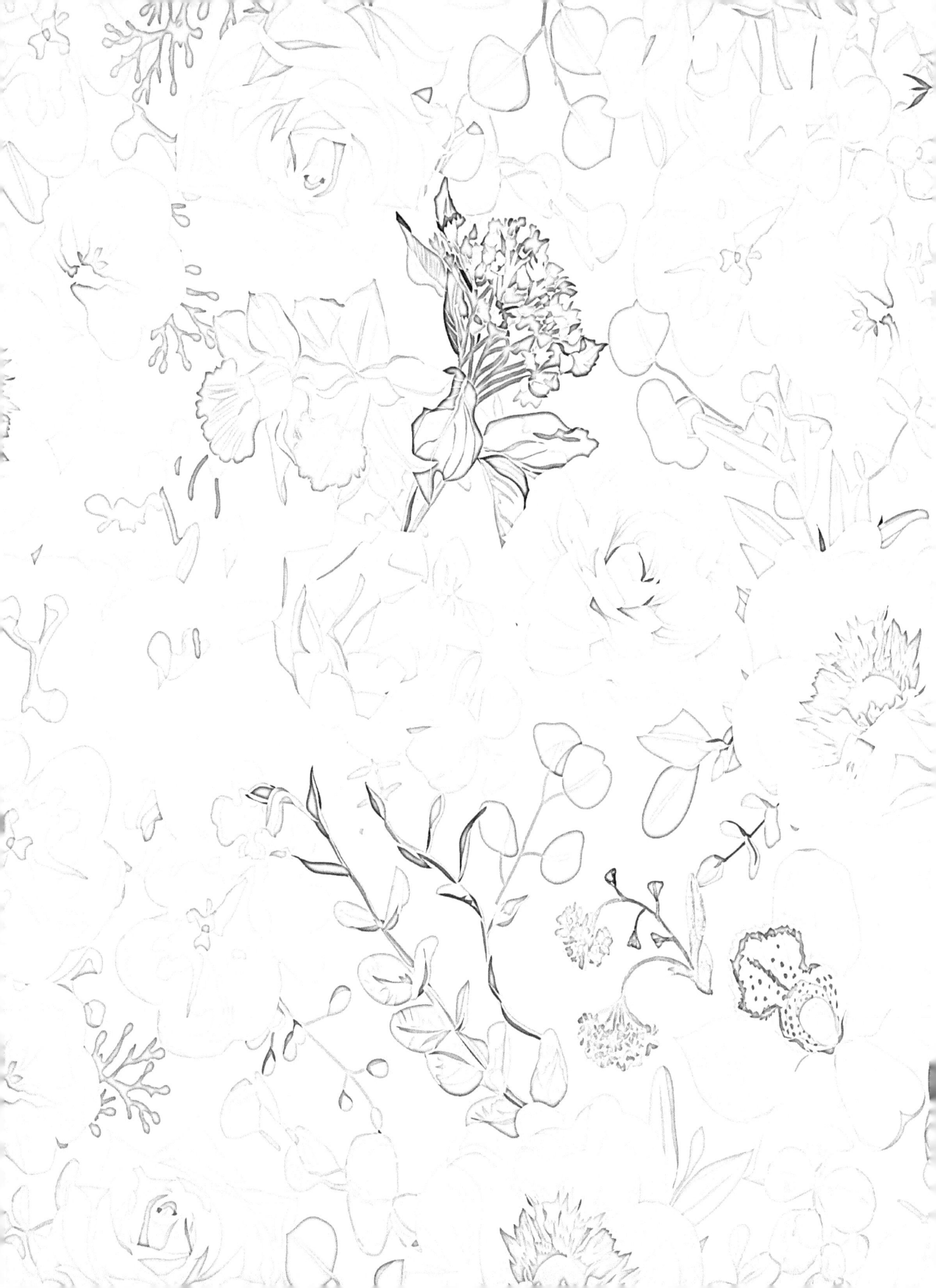

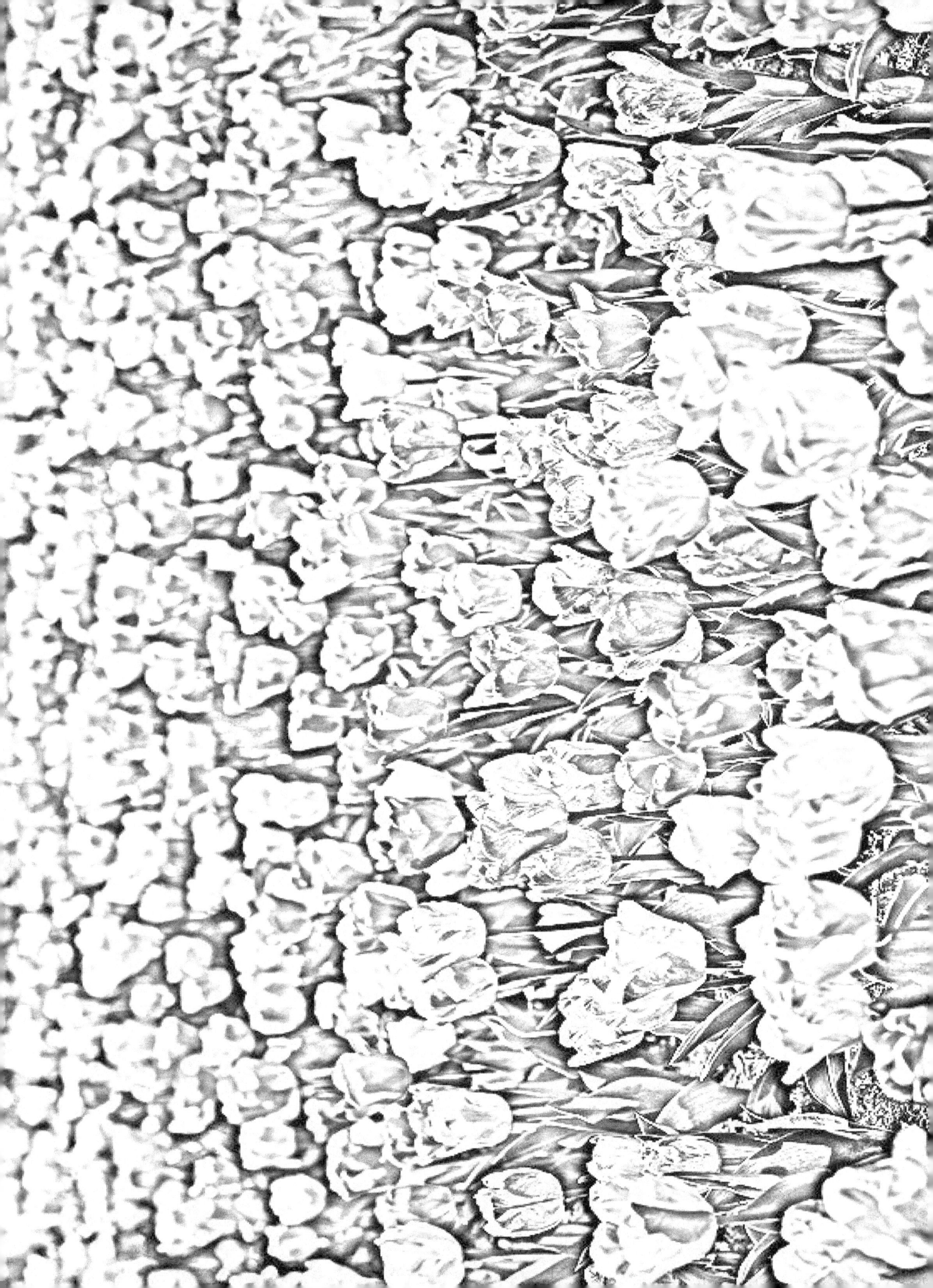

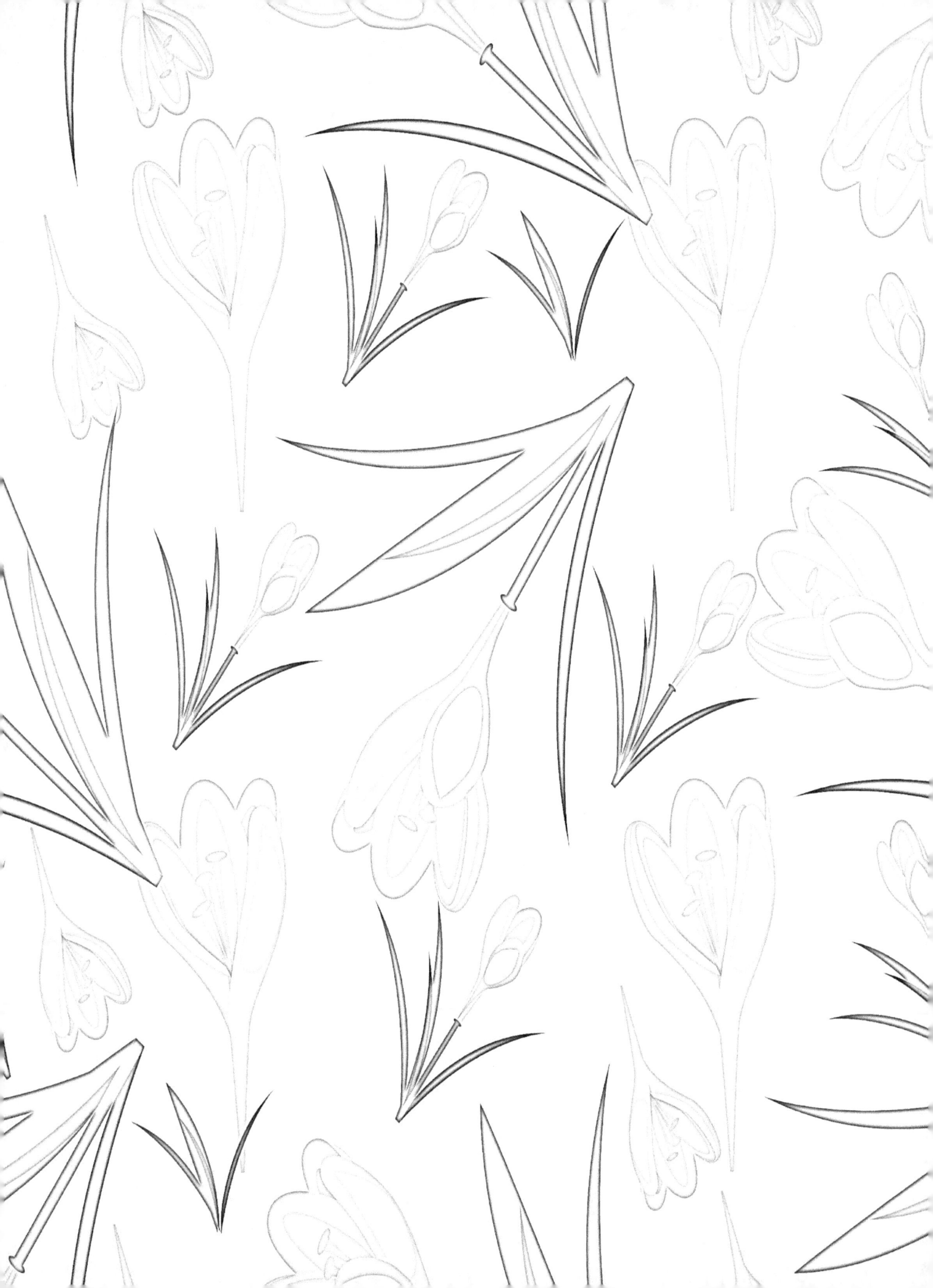

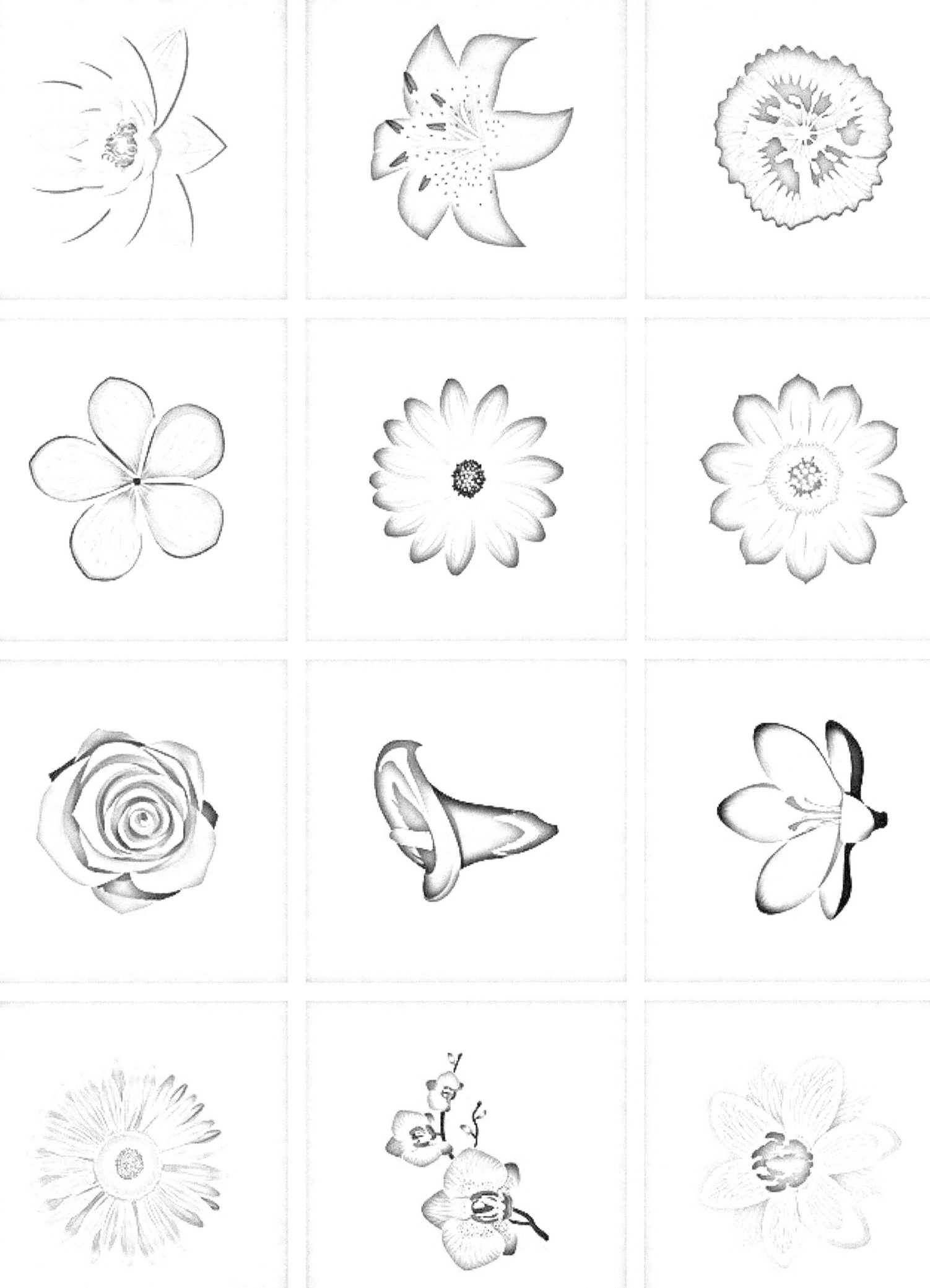

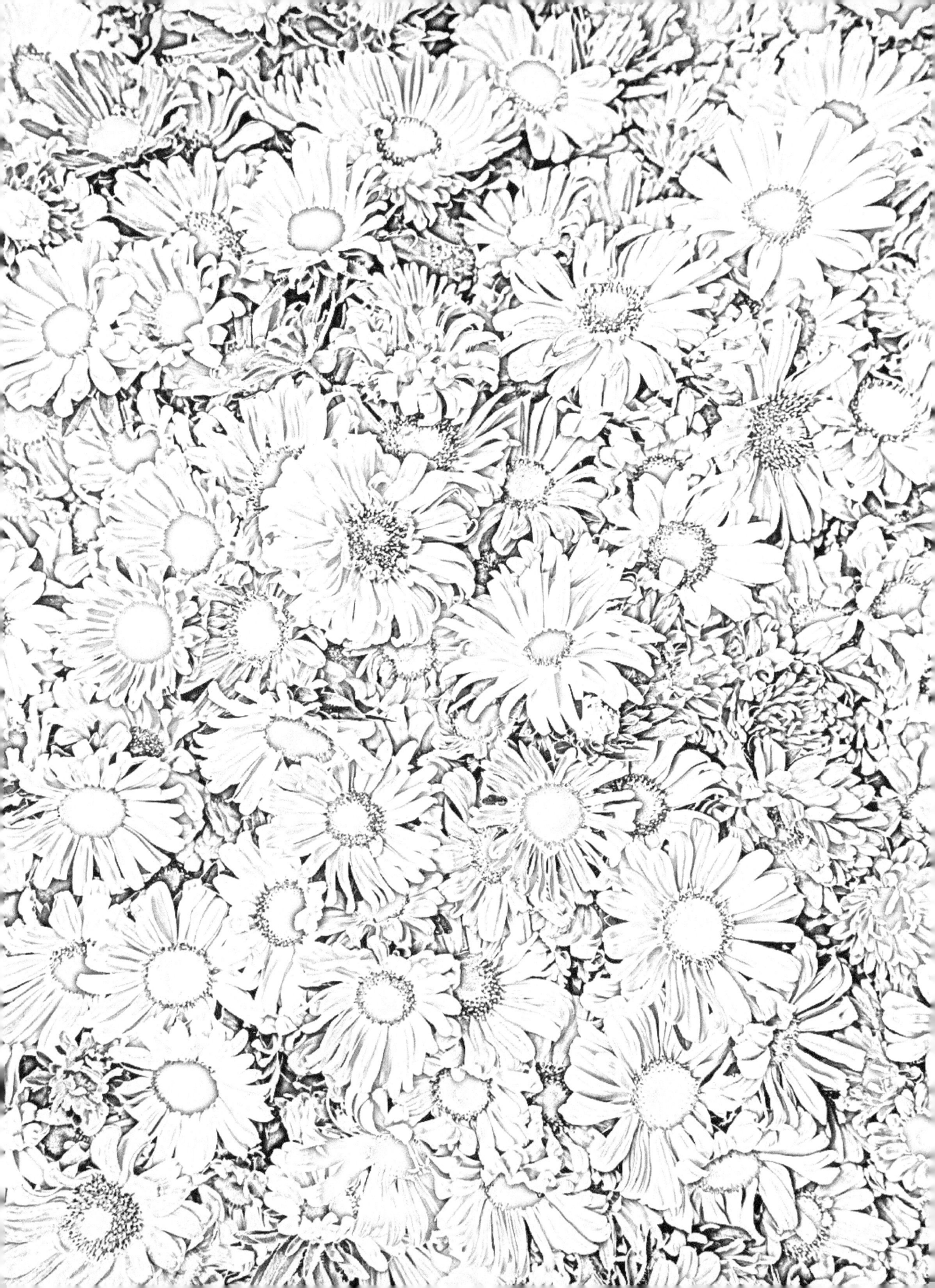

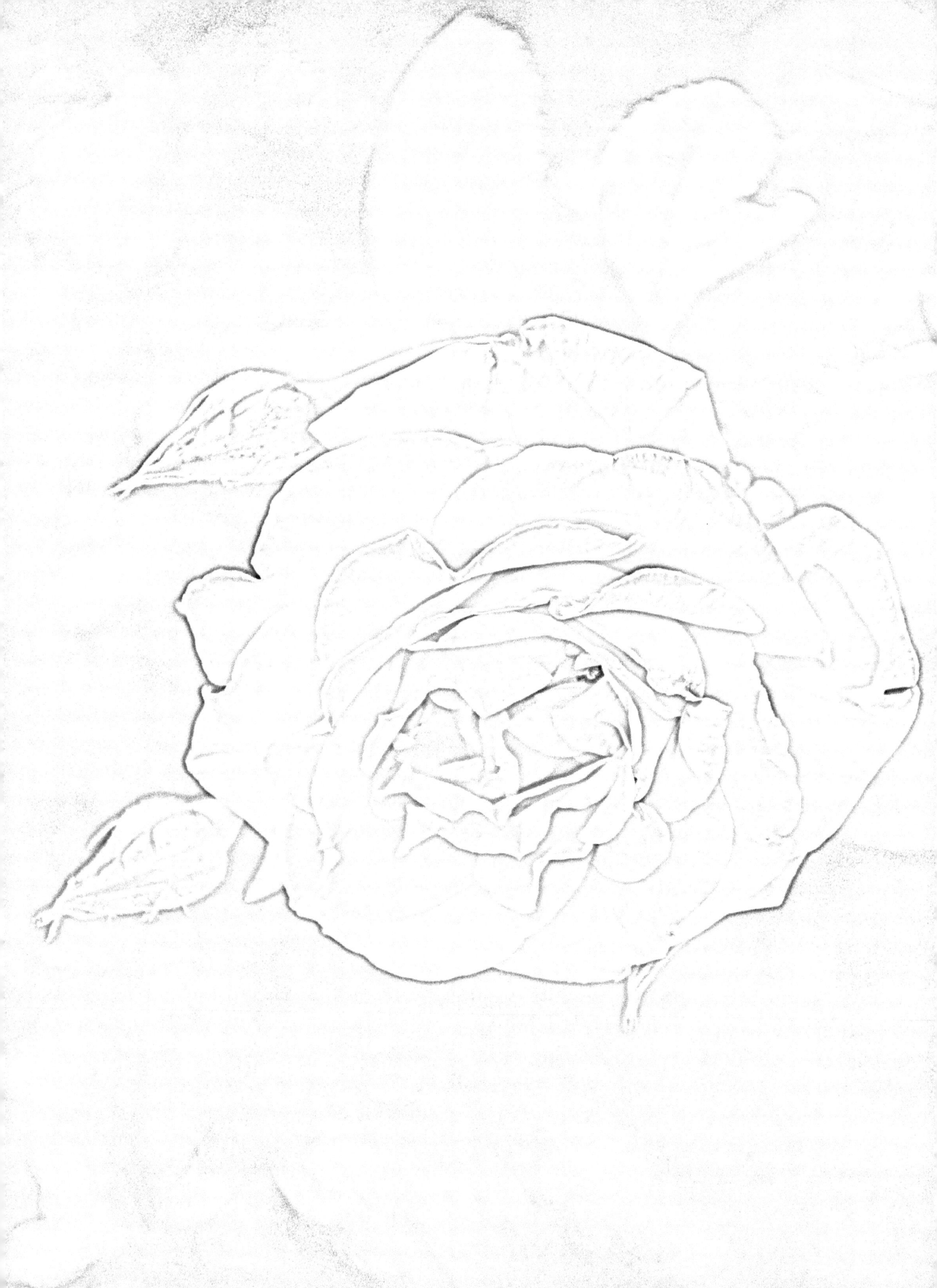

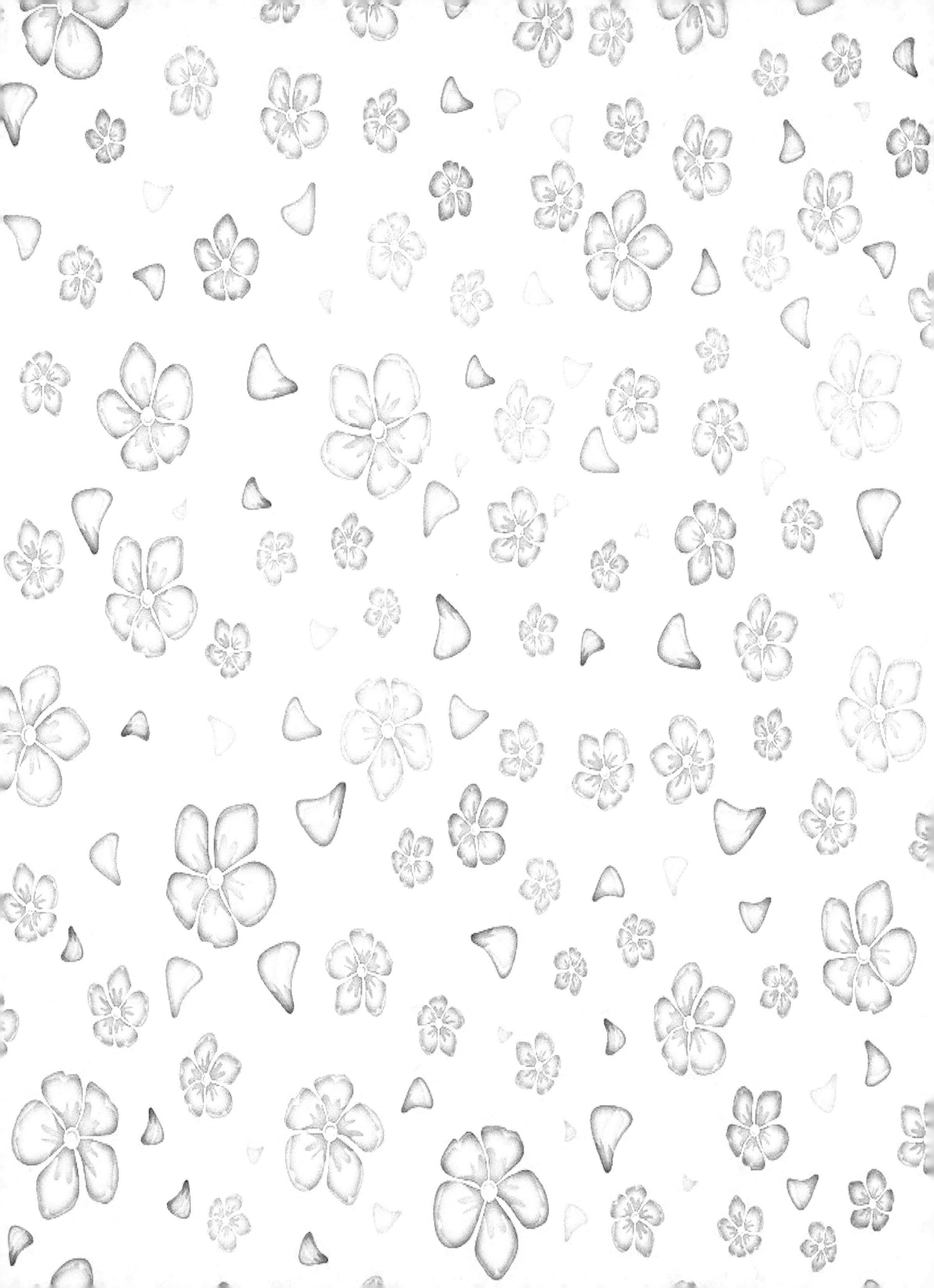

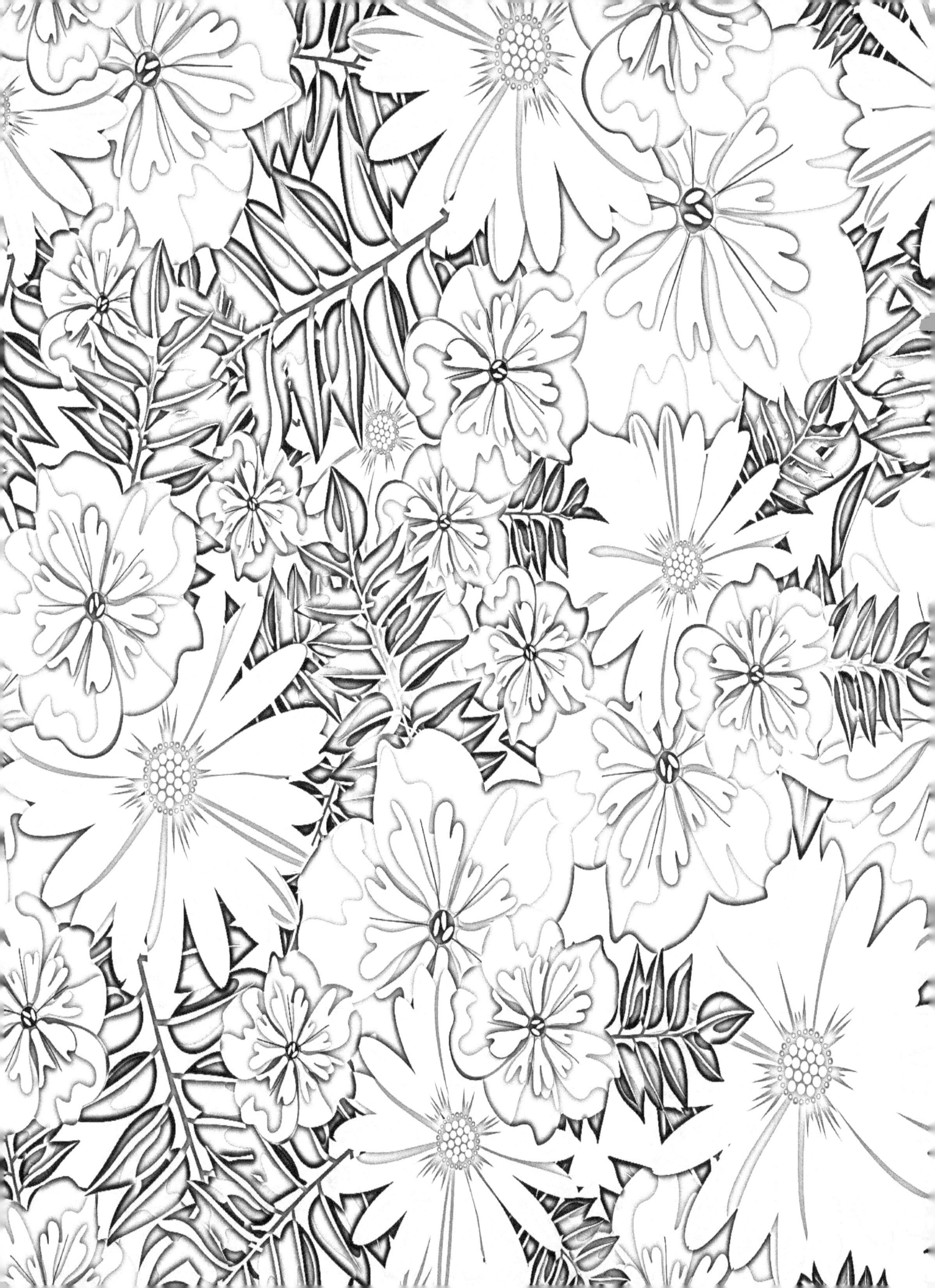

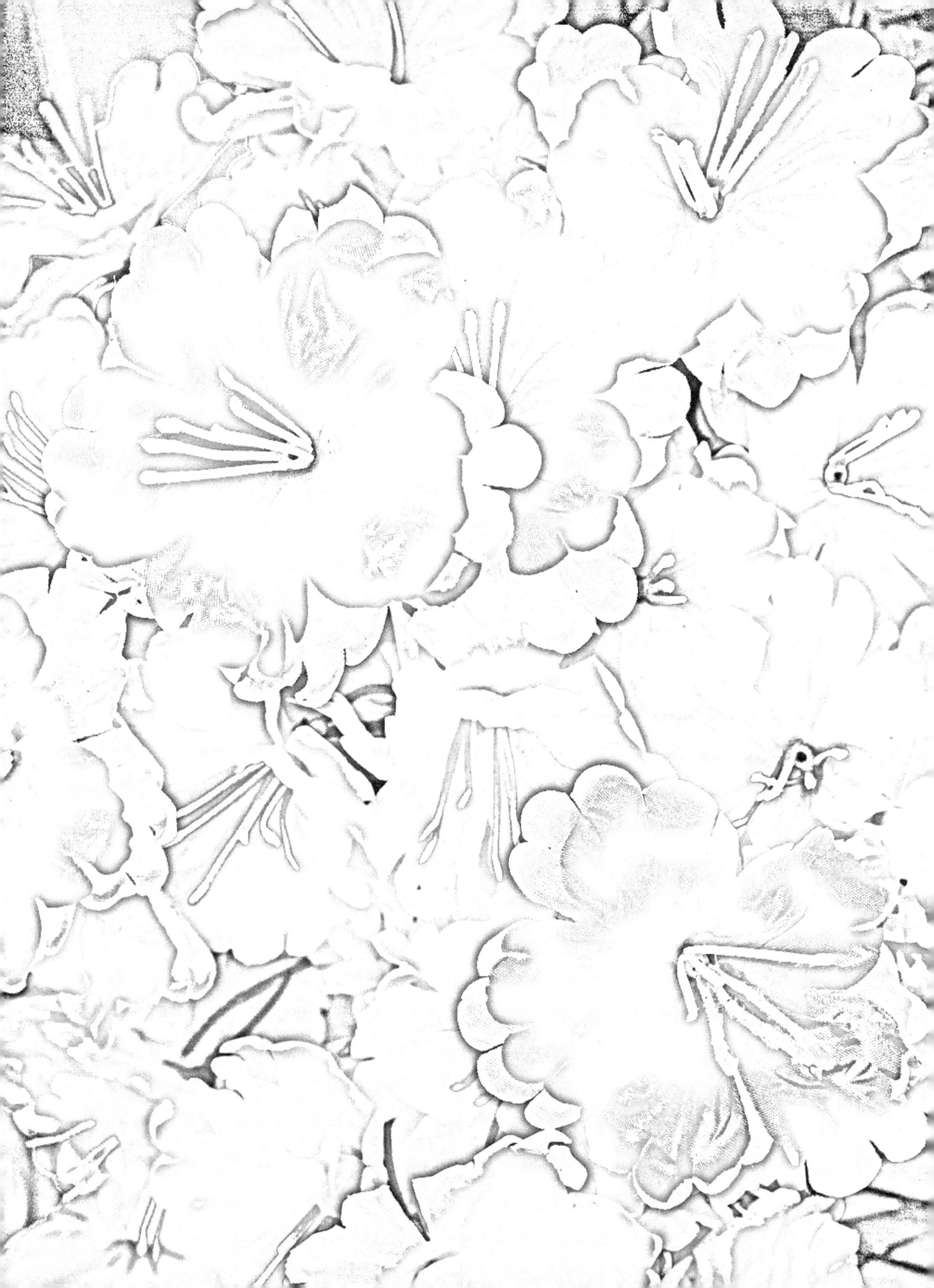

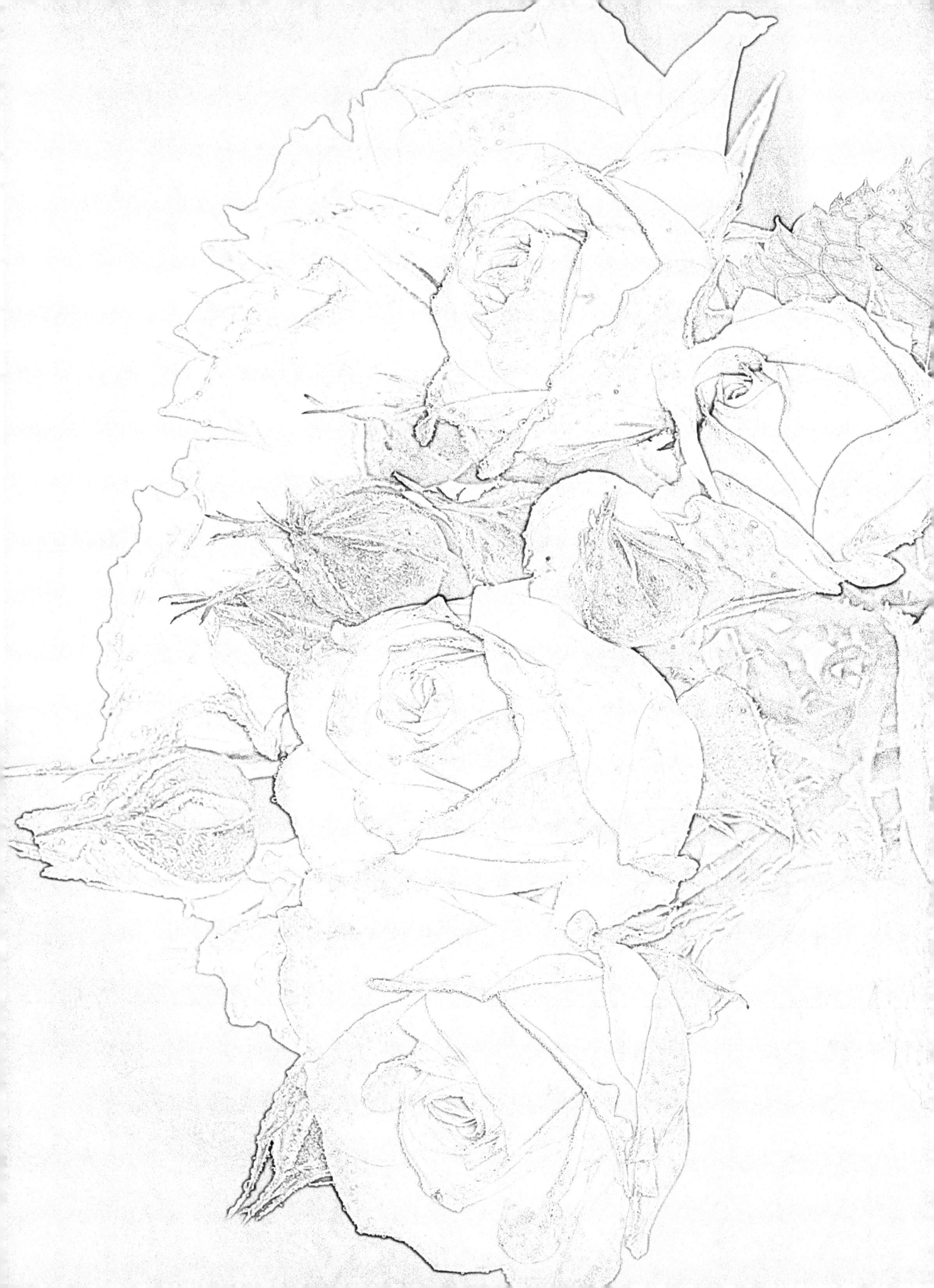

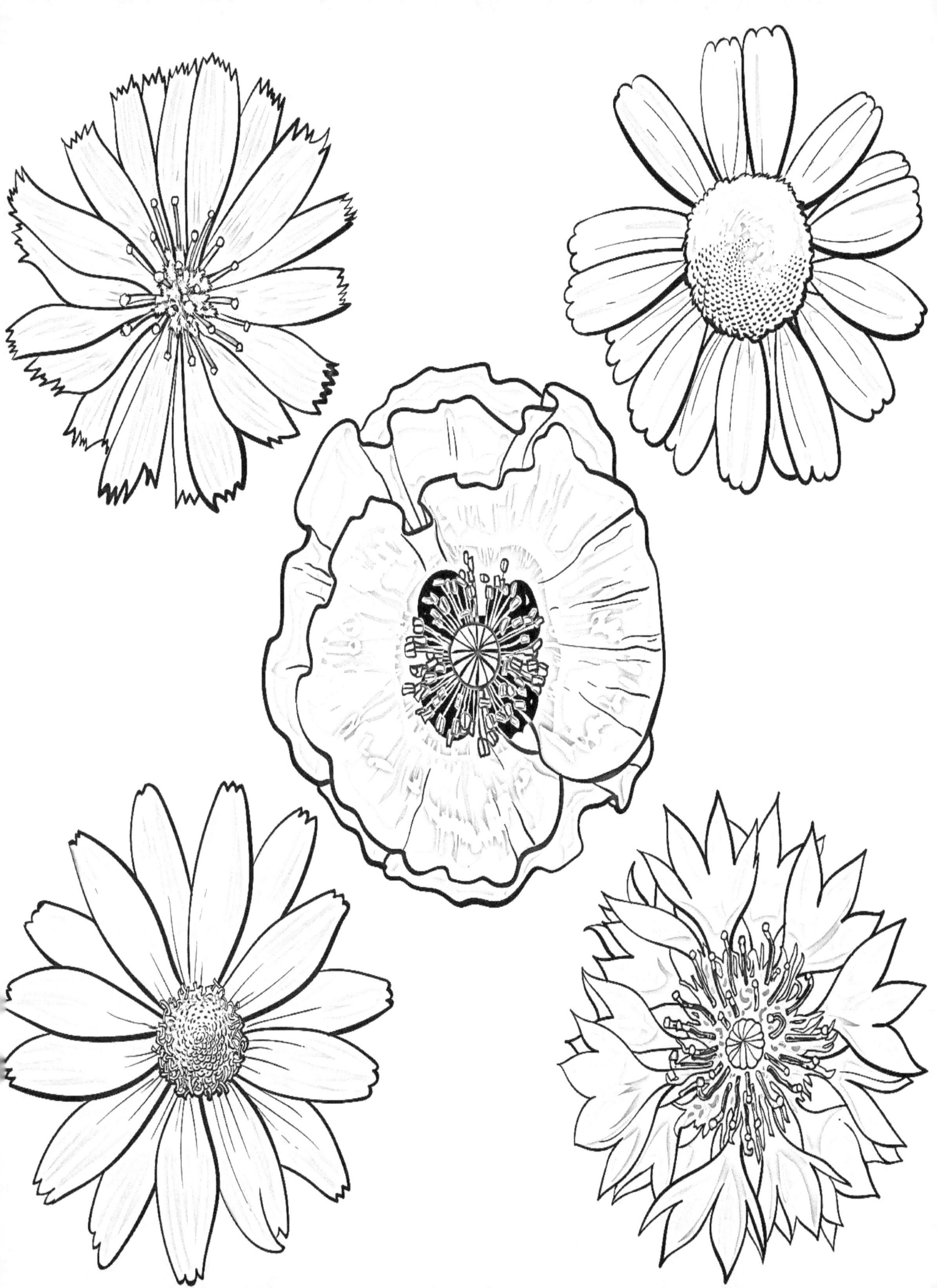

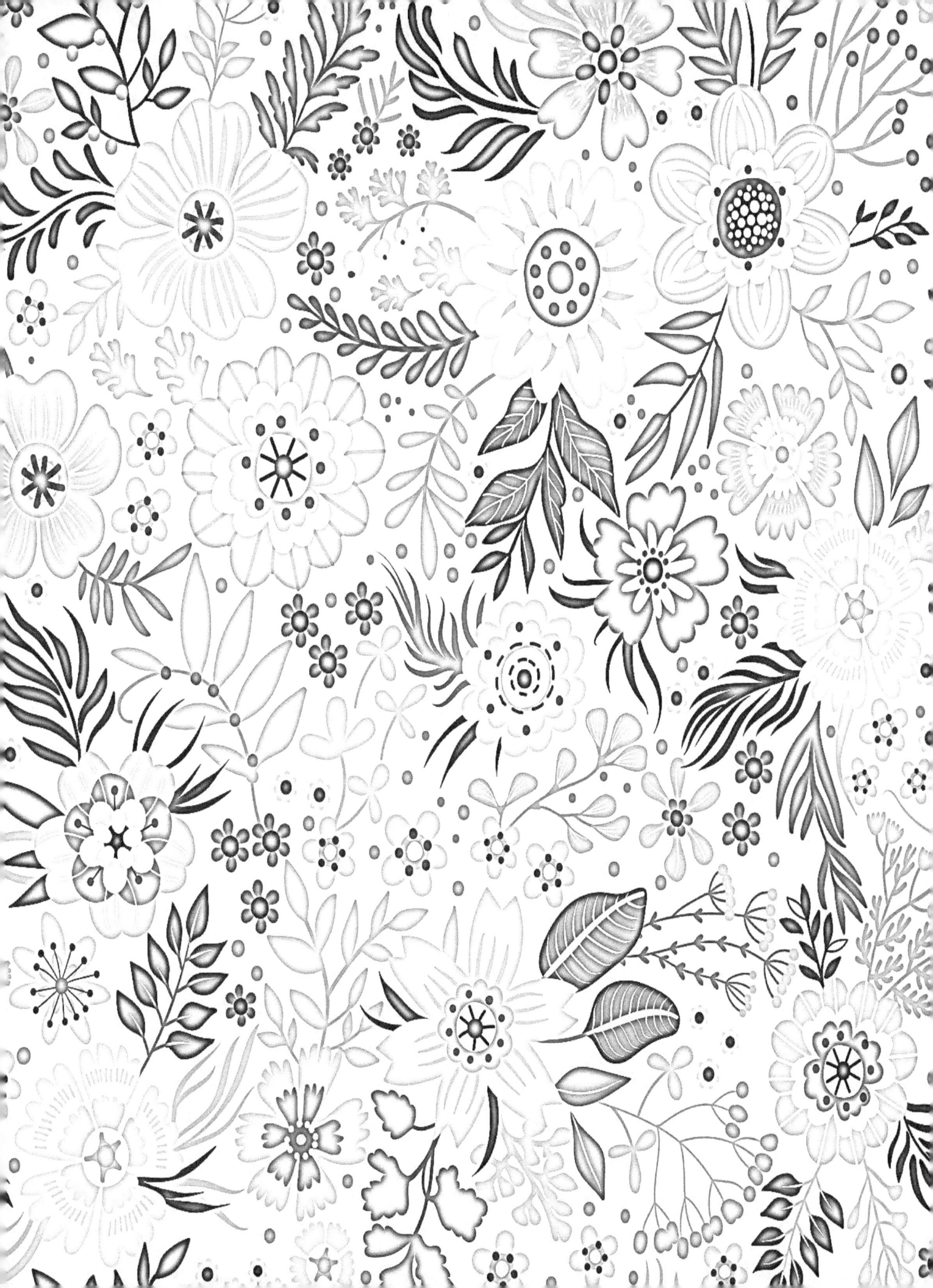

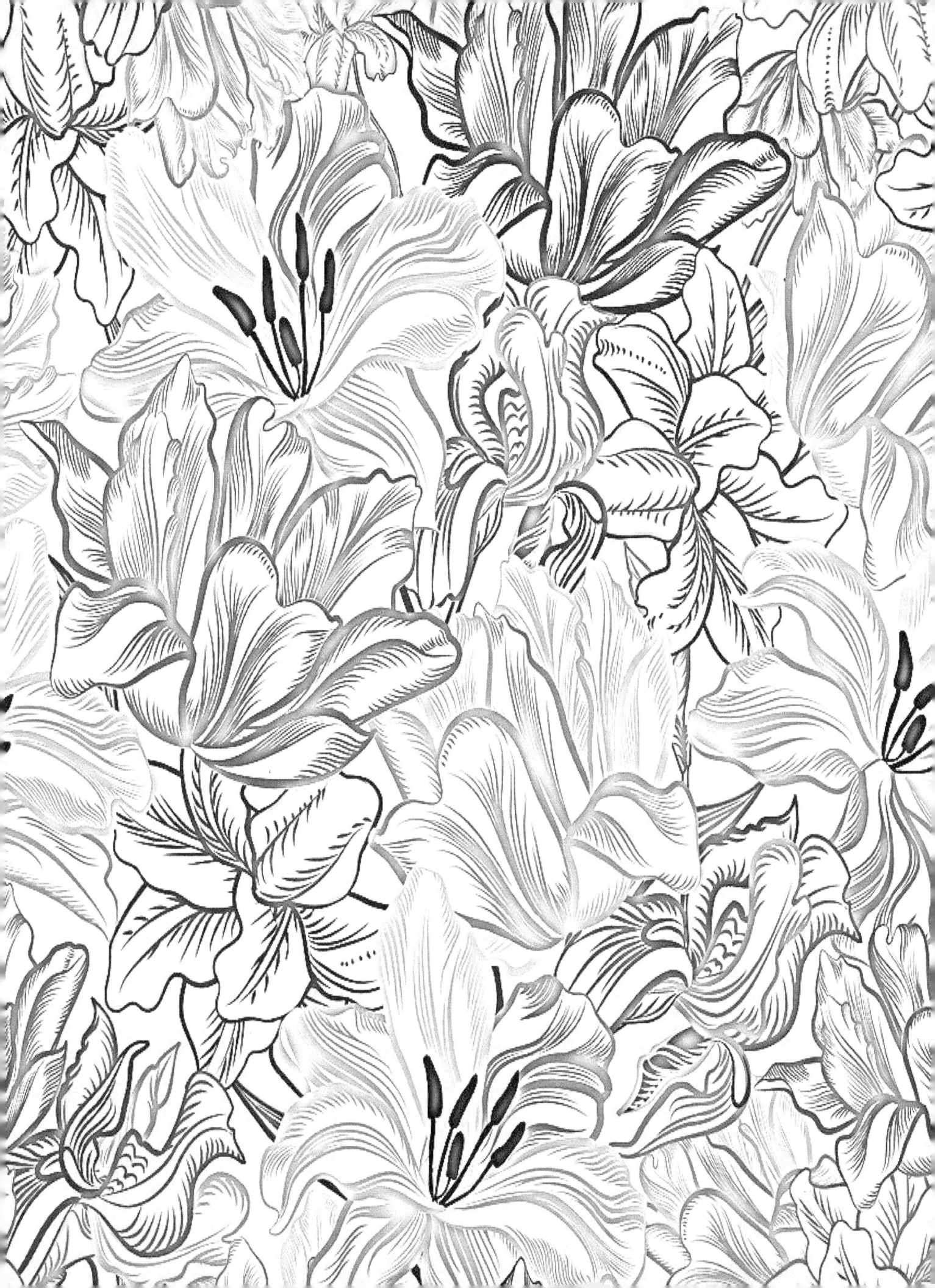

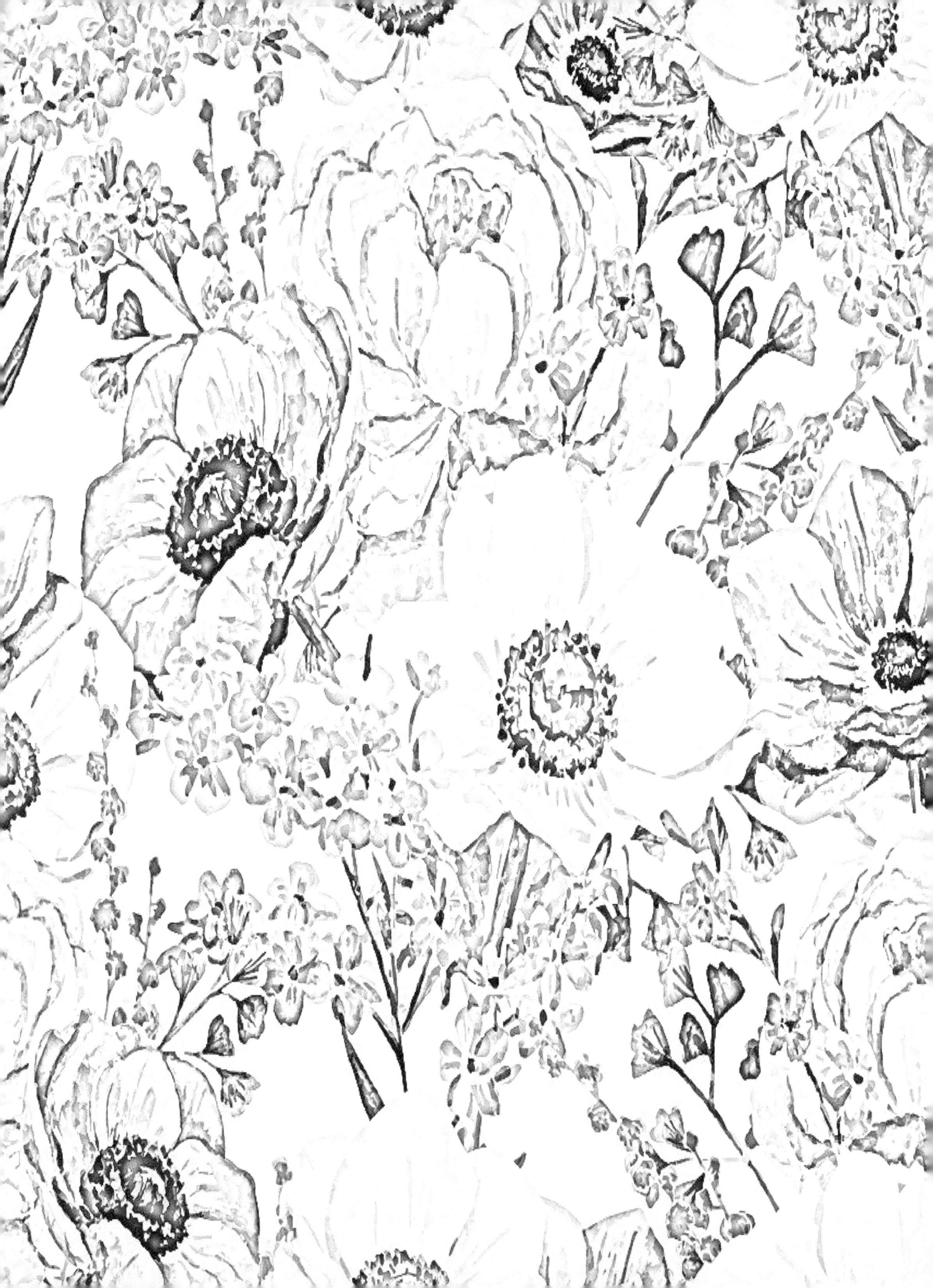

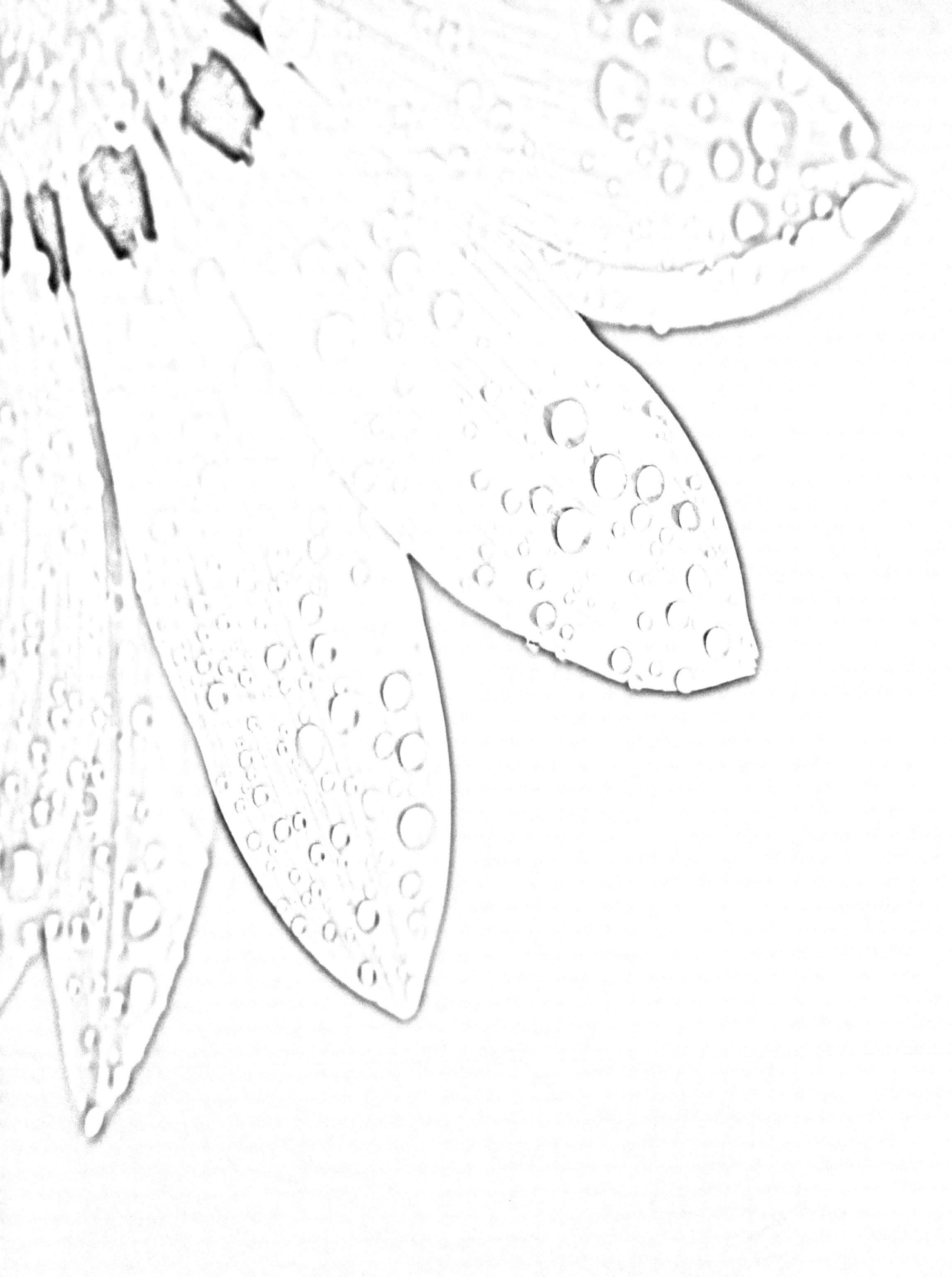

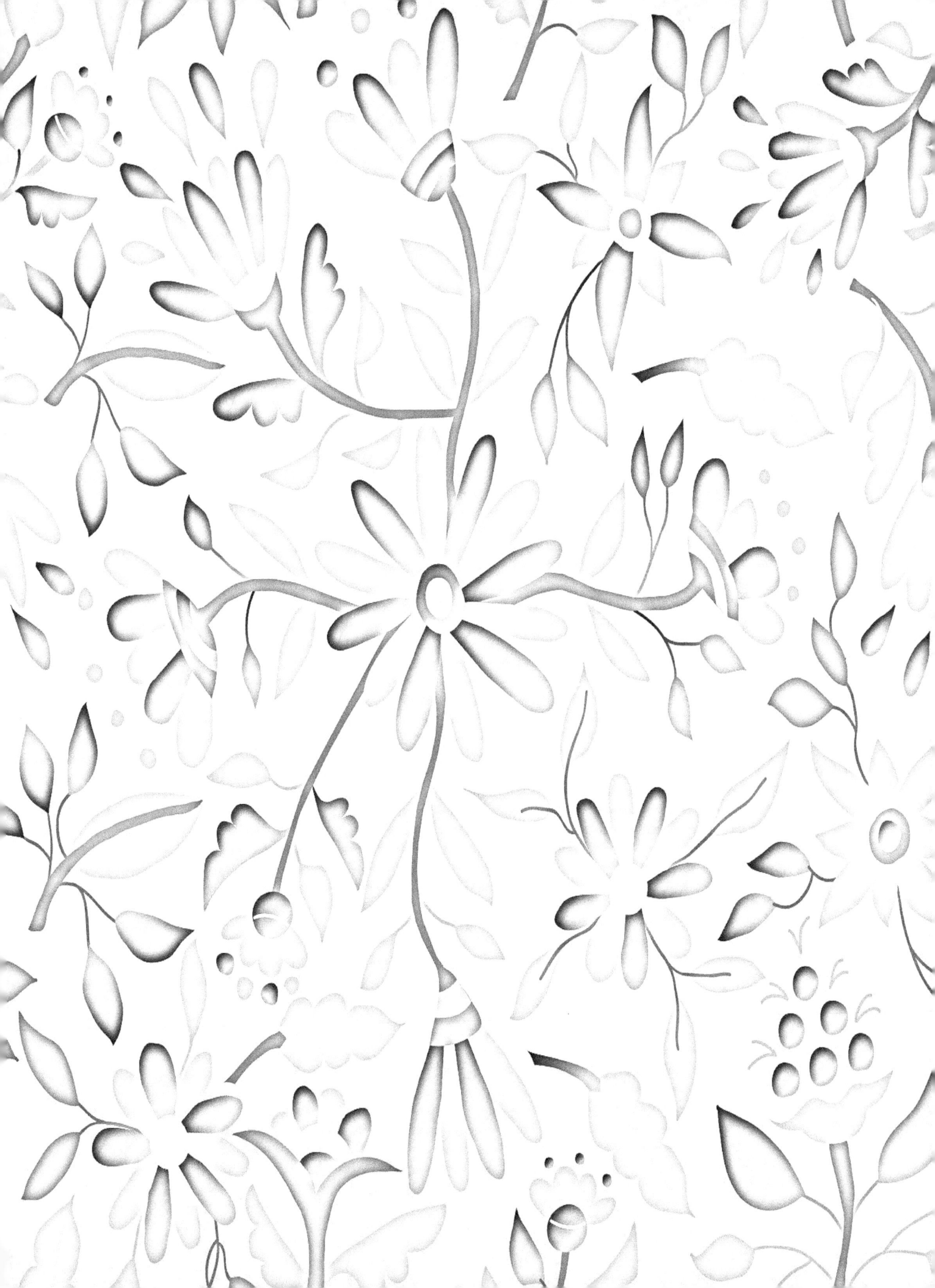

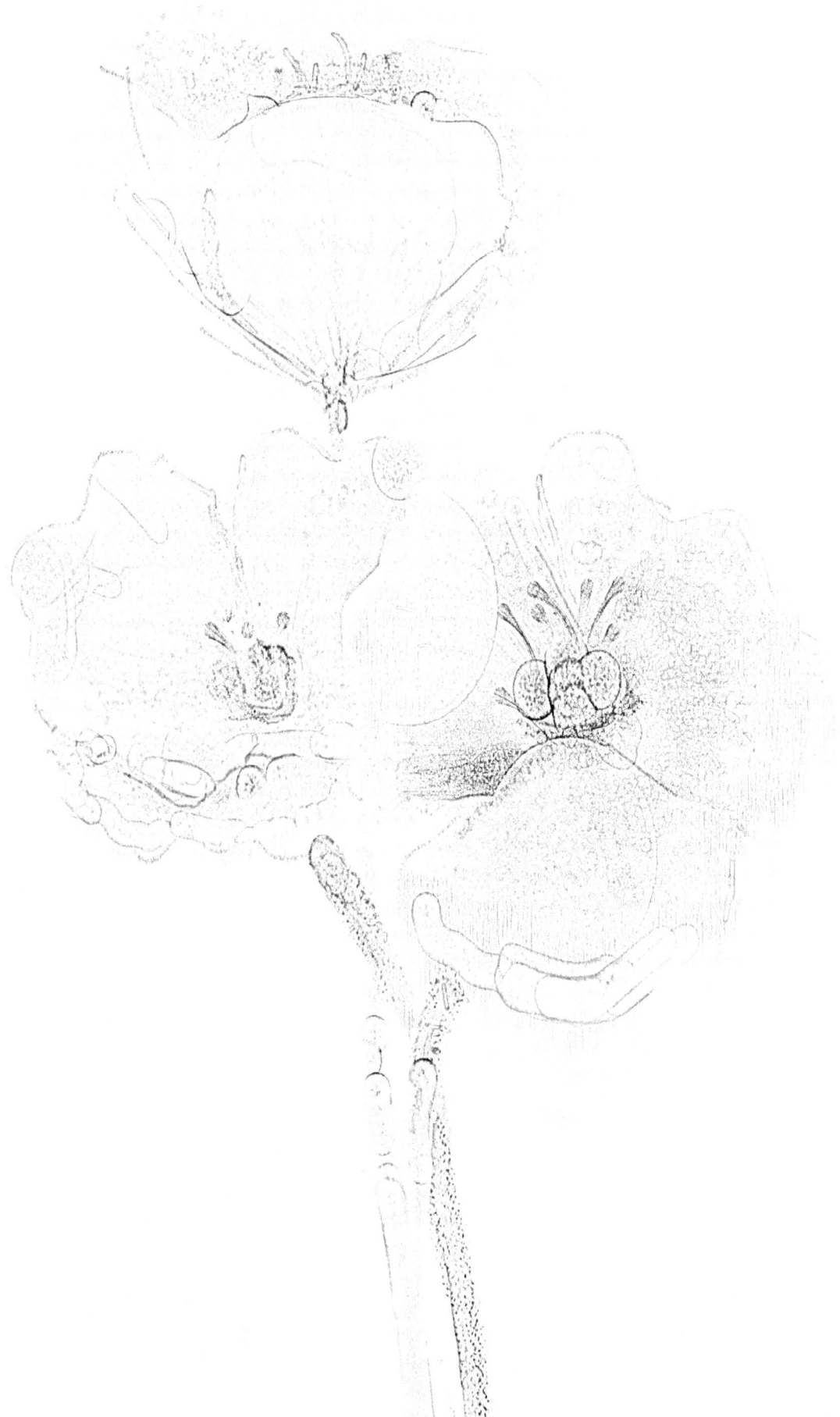

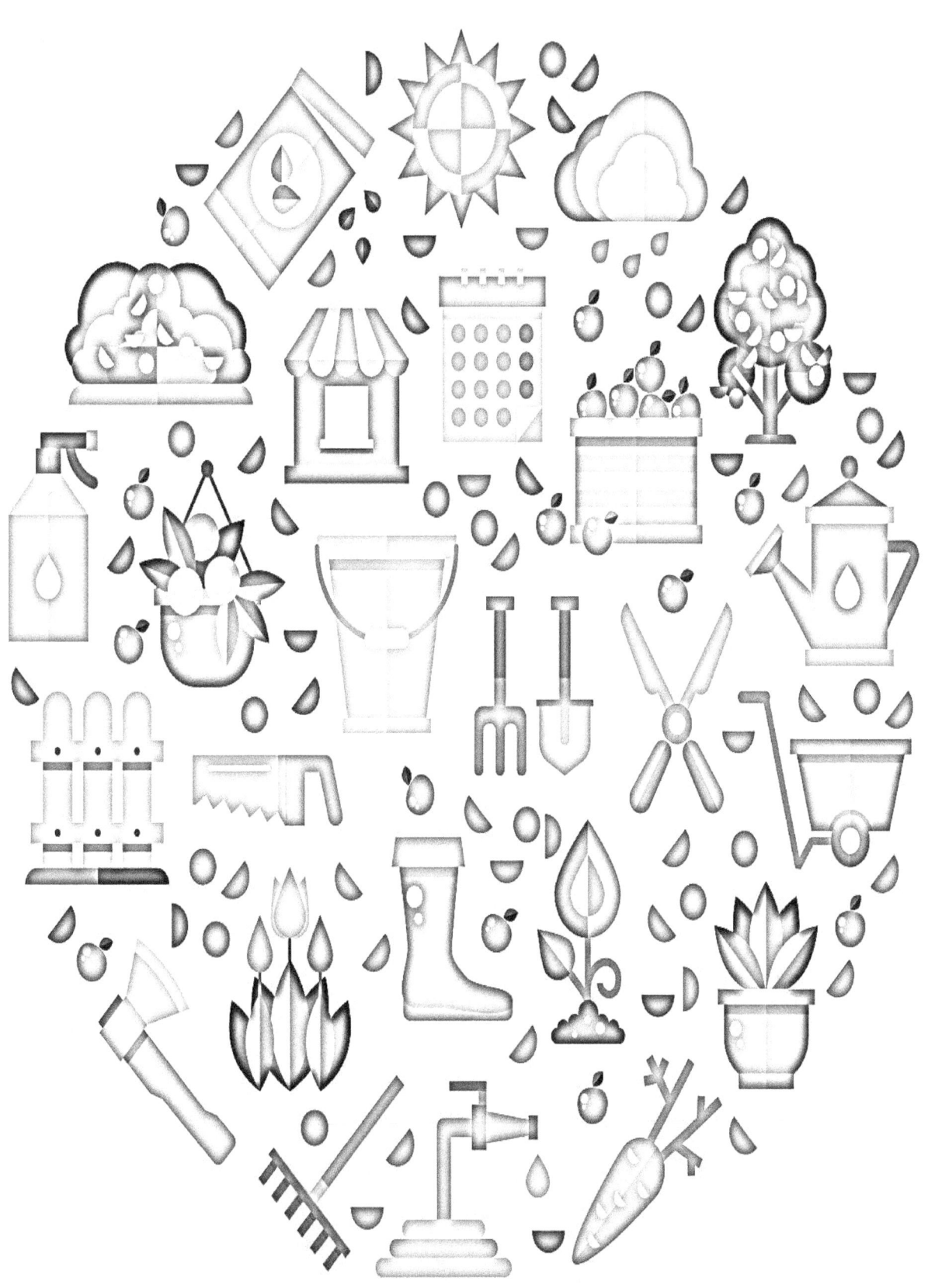

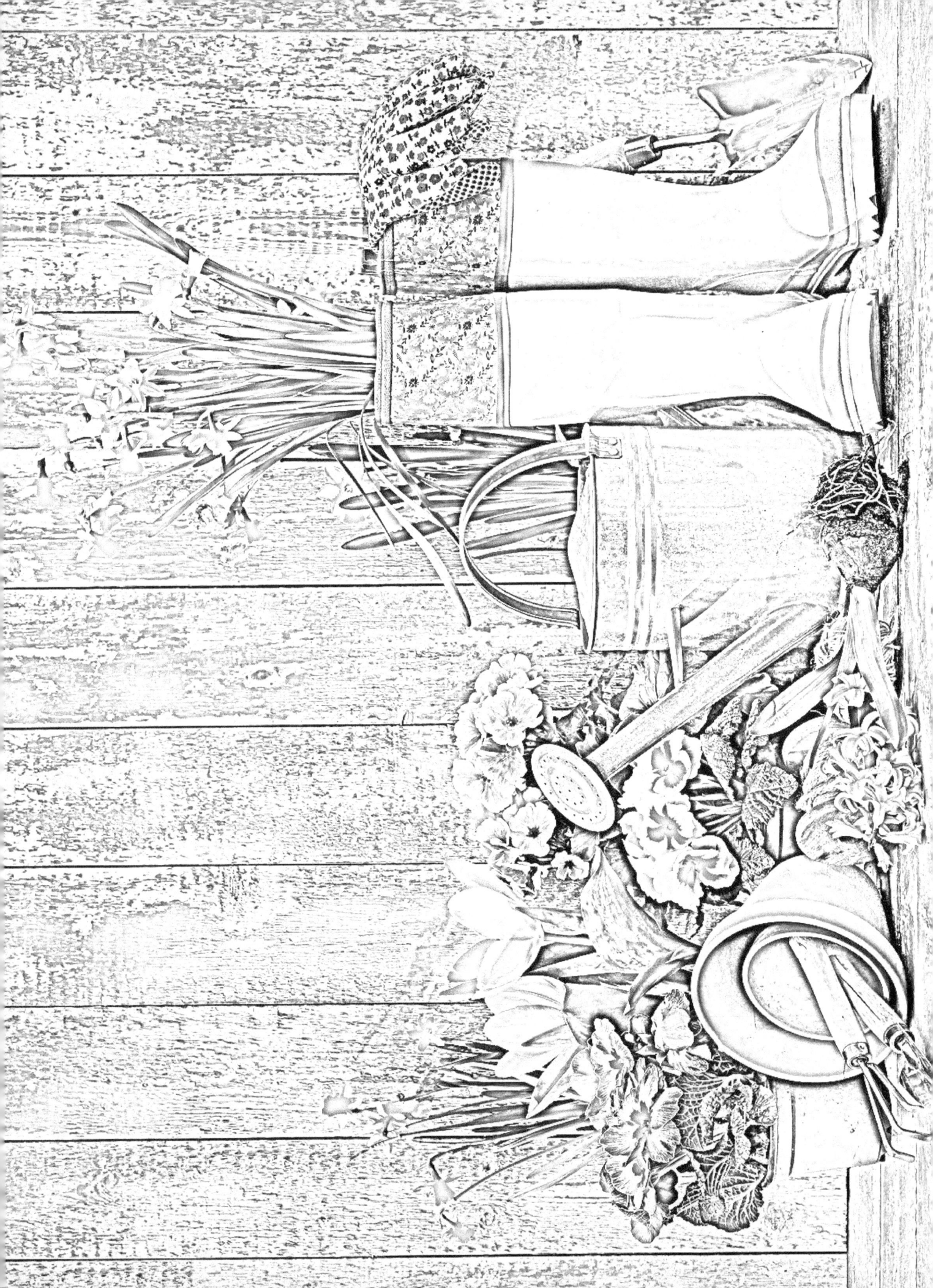

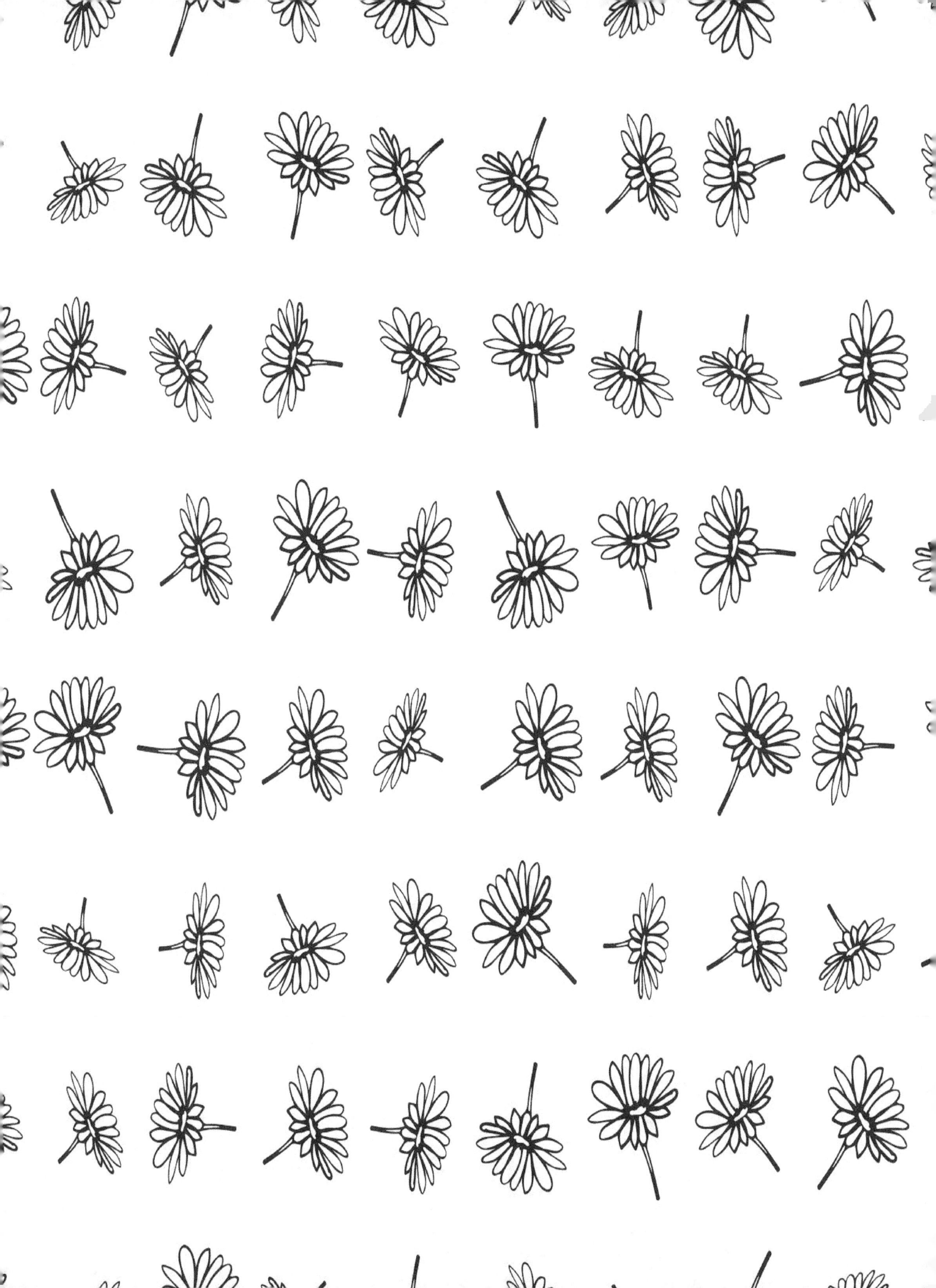

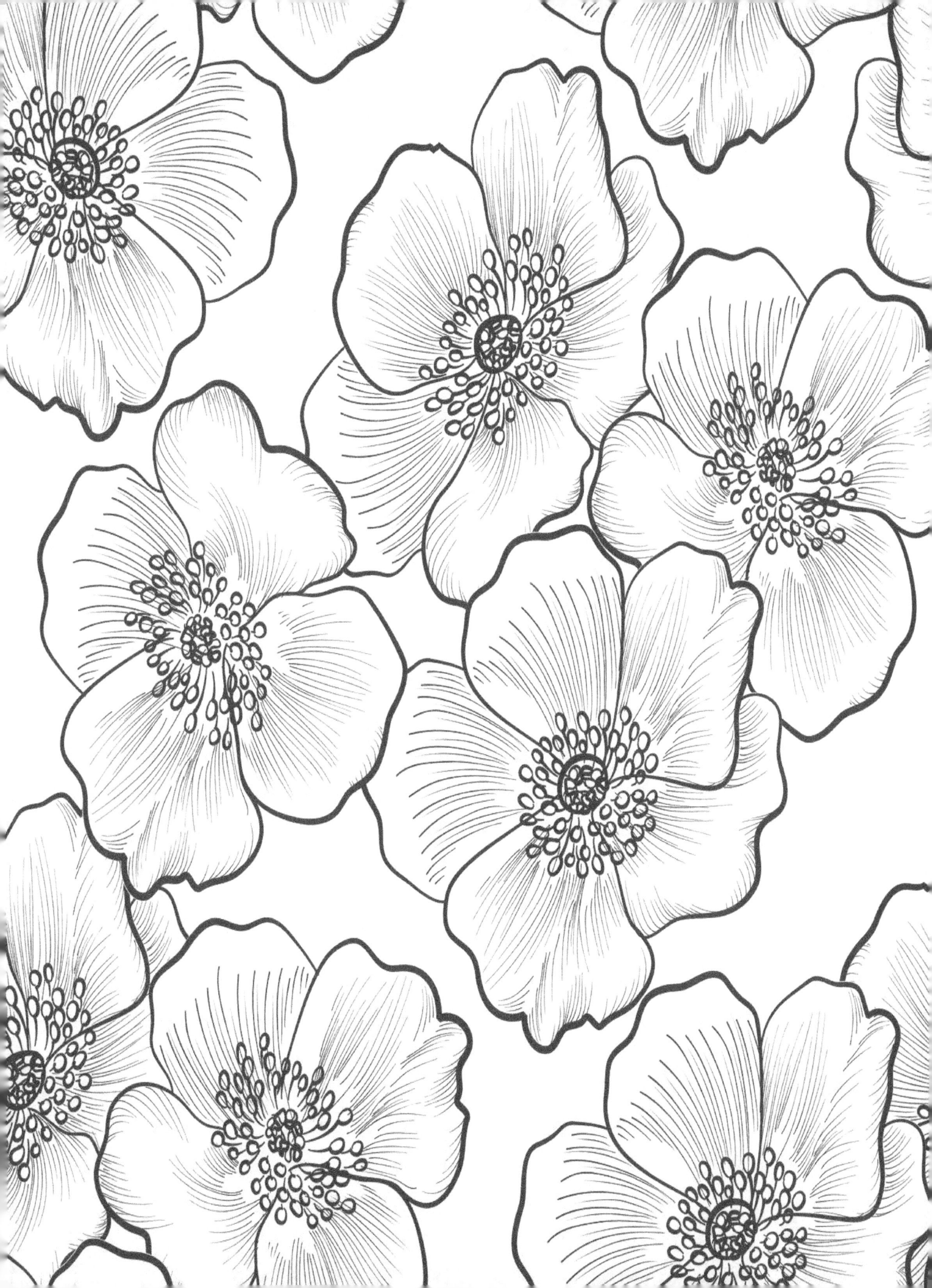

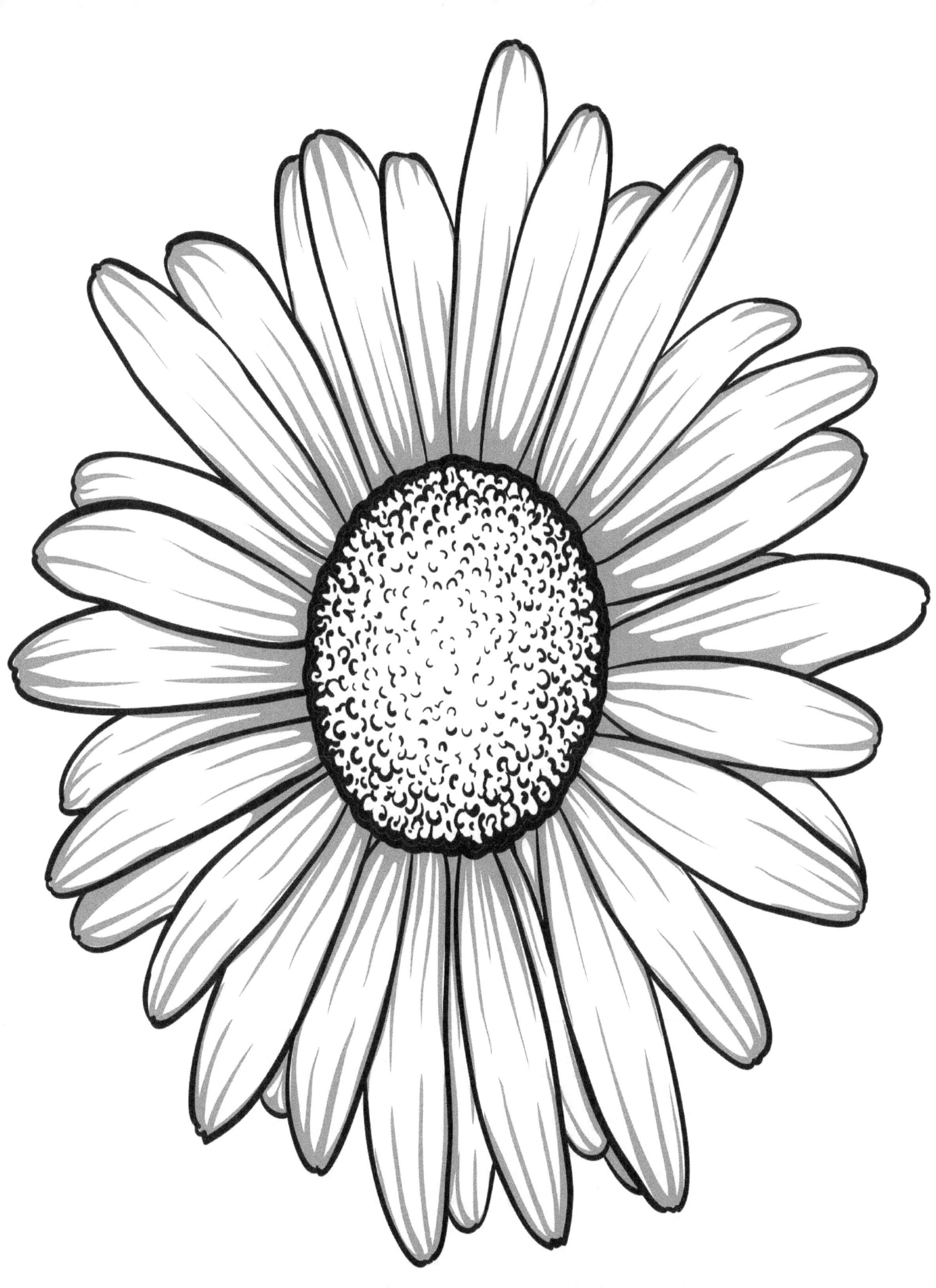

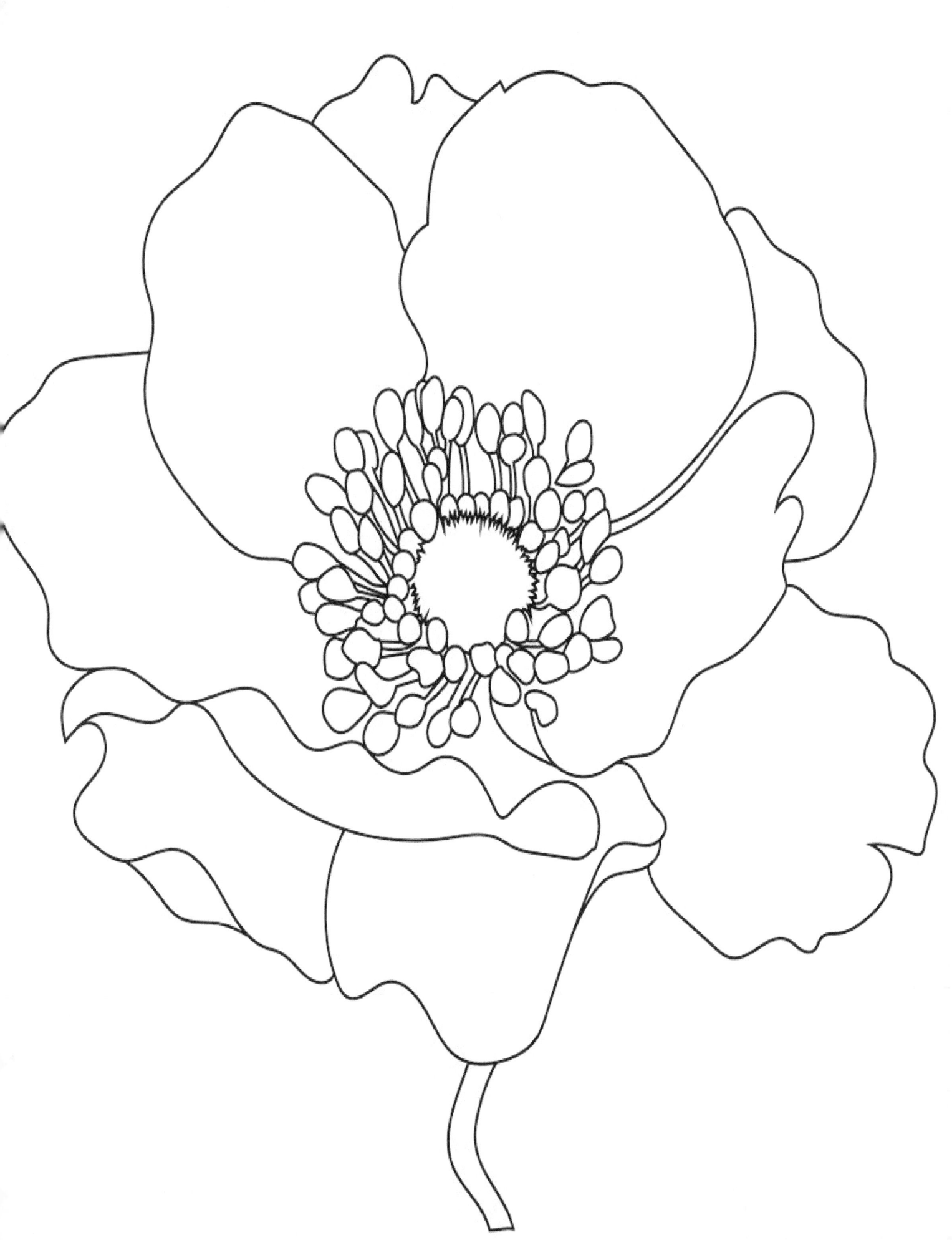

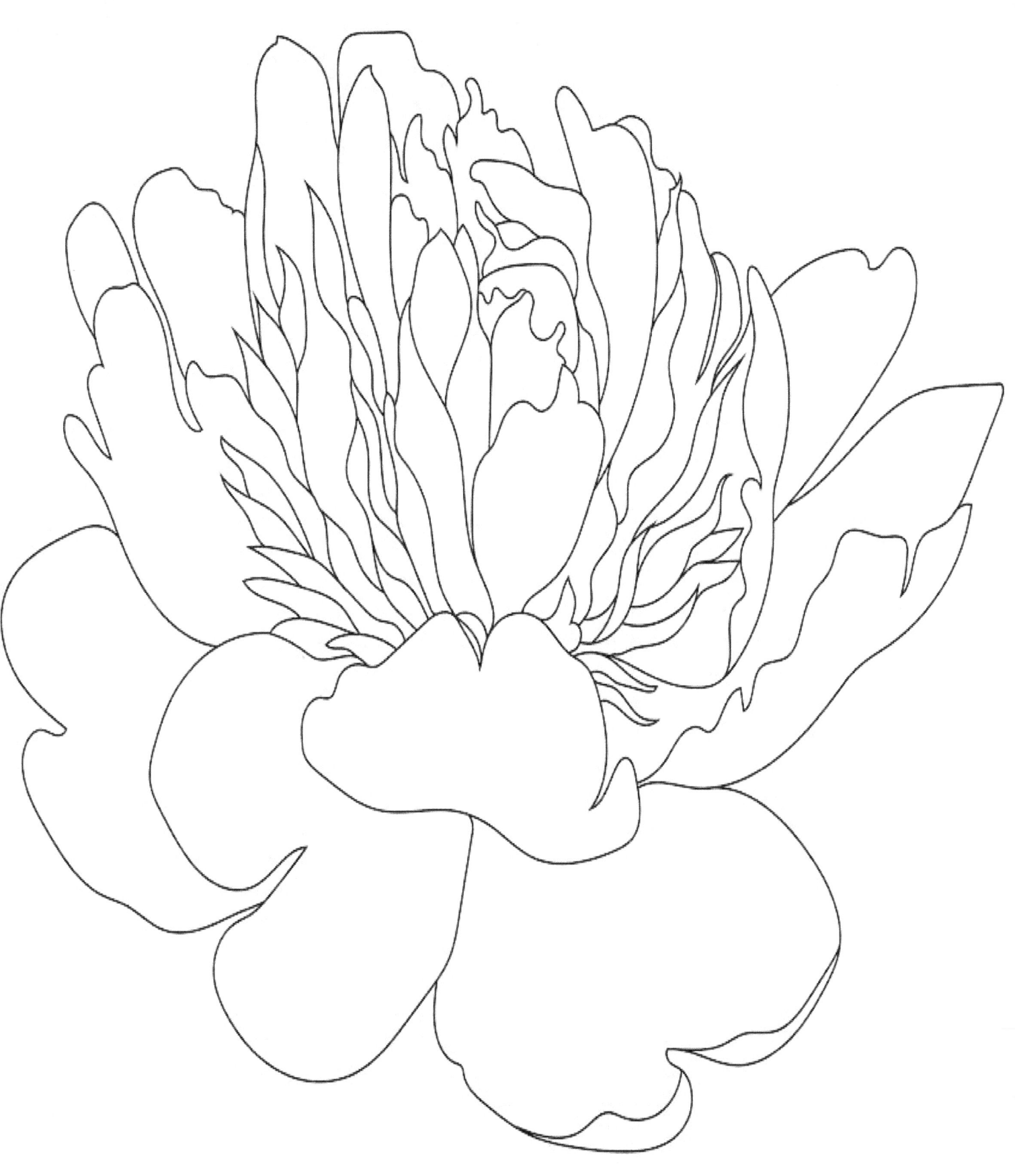

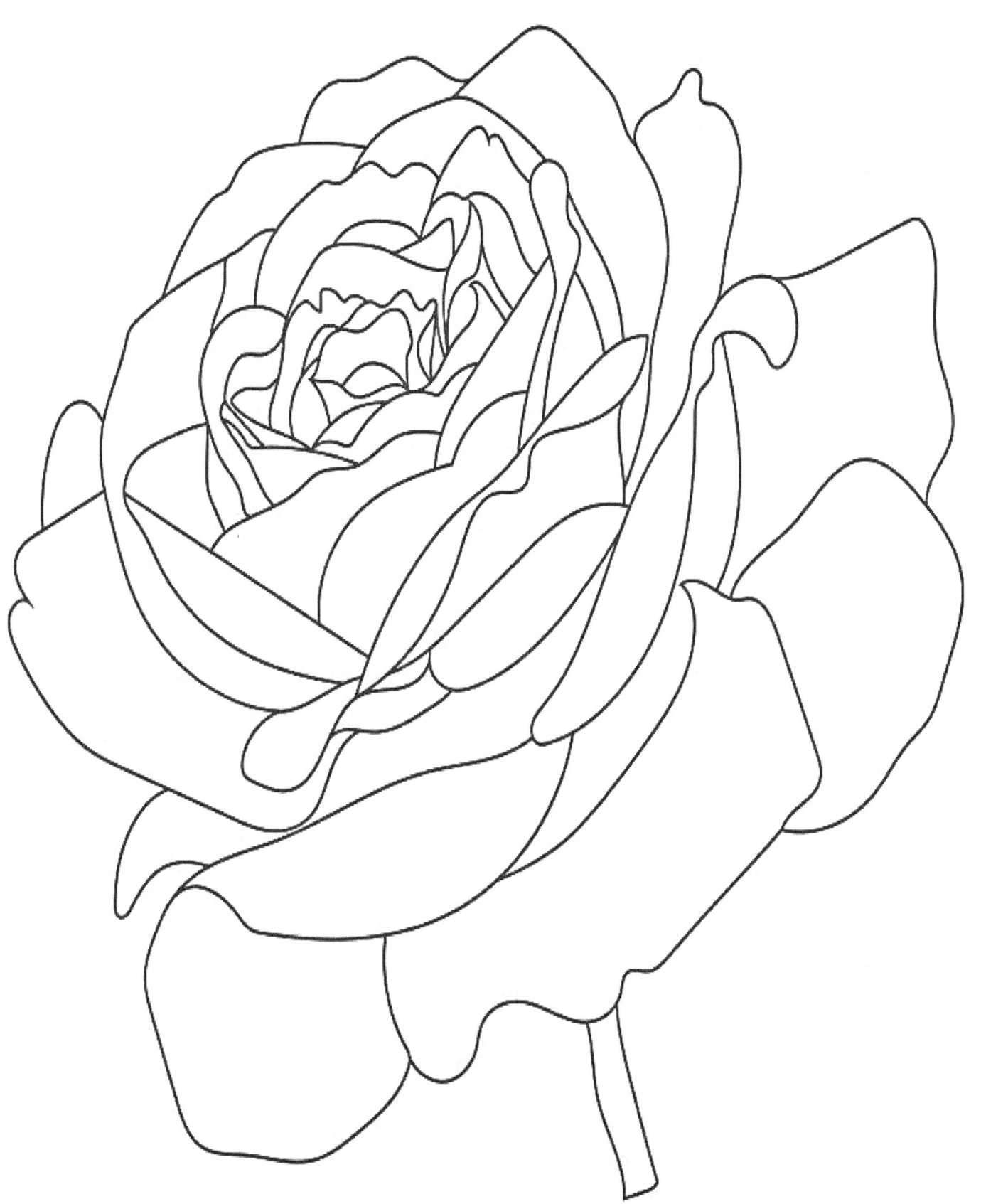

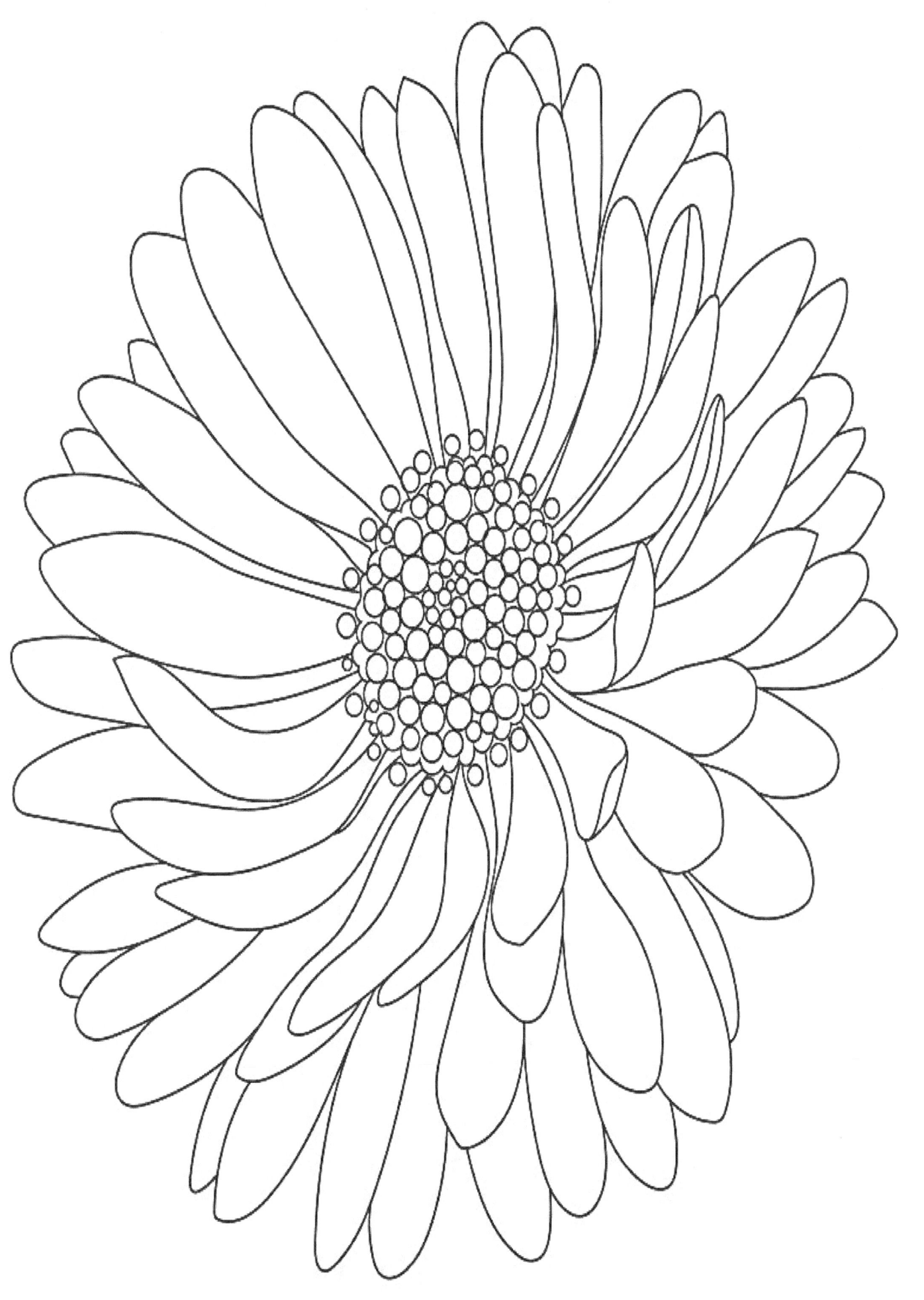

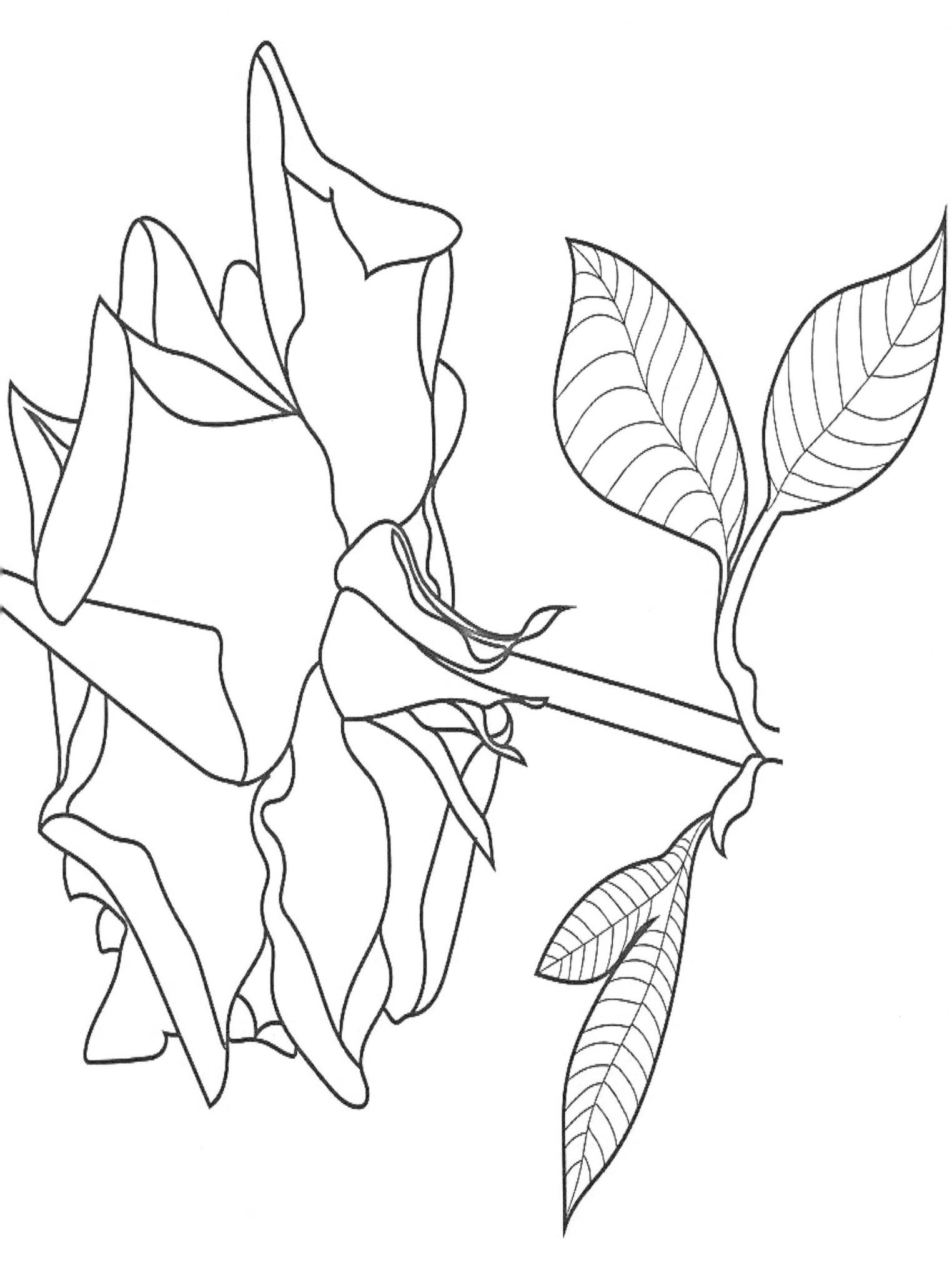

Go to http://ColoringNews.com and register for our newsletter.

We'll send info when we release new books & as our thanks we'll send you
5 additional pages to print and color!

www.ingramcontent.com/pod-product-compliance
Lightning Source LLC
Chambersburg PA
CBHW081304170526
45165CB00011B/3409